# My First
# Action
# Words
# Picture Dictionary

ENGLISH - URDU

Designed and edited by : Anna Stoker

Translated by : Dr. Amir Jamal

WIGWAM

ENGLISH - URDU

# My First
# Action Words
# Picture Dictionary

ISBN : 978 93 83526 93 2

Published by
**WigWam**
An imprint of **Star Publishers Distributors**
F-31, Okhla Industrial Area Phase I
New Delhi - 110 020
email : starprint@starpublic.com

First Edition : 2022

Printed at : Star Print-O-Bind, New Delhi-110 020 (India)

This dictionary has been published in the following languages:
Arabic, Bengali, Bulgarian, Cantonese, Croatian, Czech, Farsi, French, Gujarati, Hindi
Hungarian, Italian, Korean, Latvian, Levantine, Lithuanian, Mandarin, Pashto, Polish, Portuguese
Punjabi, Romanian, Russian, Slovak, Spanish, Tamil, Urdu and Vietnamese.

# Aa

## abandon

chhorna      چھوڑنا

## absent

ghair haazir hona      غیر حاضر ہونا

## absorb

jazb karna      جذب کرنا

## accelerate

tez tar karna      تیز تر کرنا

## accept

qubool karna      قبول کرنا

## access

rasaai      رسائی

## accompany

saath jaana      ساتھ جانا

## accuse

ilzaam lagaana      الزام لگانا

## ache

dard karna      درد کرنا

## achieve

paana      پانا

## acquire

haasil karna      حاصل کرنا

## act

adakaari karna      اداکاری کرنا

## add

ملانا،اضافہ کرنا
milaana, izaafa karna

## adjust

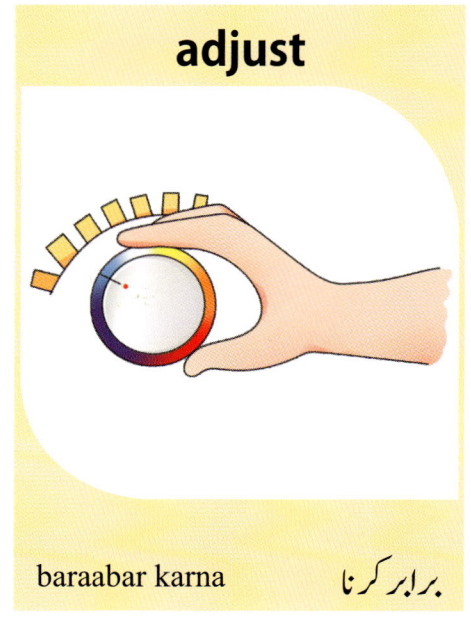

baraabar karna      برابر کرنا

## admire

pasand karna      پسند کرنا

## admit

daakhil karna      داخل کرنا

## adopt

god lena      گود لینا

## adore

mohabbat karna محبت کرنا

## advance

aage barhna آگے بڑھنا

## advise

salaah dena صلاح دینا

## affix

chipkaana چپکانا

## afford

استطاعت رکھنا
istataat rakhna

## agree

muttafiq hona متفق ہونا

## aid

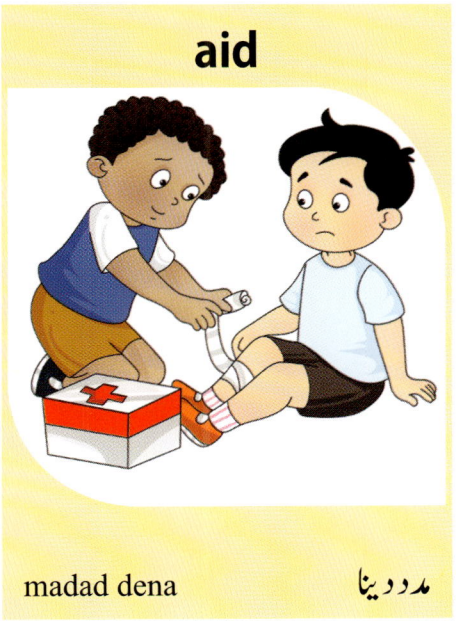

madad dena مدد دینا

## aim

نشانہ سادھنا
nishaana saadhna

## align

seedh mein karna سیدھ میں کرنا

### allow

ijaazat dena     اجازت دینا

### alter

tabdeel karna     تبدیل کرنا

### amaze

hairaan karna     حیران کرنا

### amuse

dil khush karna     دل خوش کرنا

### analyse

*US English* **analyze**

tajziya karna     تجزیہ کرنا

### anger

ghussa karna     غُصّہ کرنا

### announce

ilaan karna     اعلان کرنا

### annoy

pareshaan karna     پریشان کرنا

### answer

jawaab dena     جواب دینا

### apologise
US English **apologize**

mazrat karna     معذرت کرنا

### appear

zaahir hona     ظاہر ہونا

### applaud

waah waah kehna     واہ واہ کہنا

### apply

lagaana     لگانا

### appoint

mutayyan karna     متعین کرنا

### approach

paas aana     پاس آنا

### approve

manzoor karna     منظور کرنا

### argue

دلیل دینا، بحث کرنا
daleel dena, bahas karna

### arise

اٹھنا، کھڑے ہونا
uthna, khade hona

## arrange

tarteeb dena     ترتیب دینا

## arrest

giraftaar karna     گرفتار کرنا

## arrive

pohanchna     پہنچنا

## ask

poochhna     پُوچھنا

## assemble

jama hona     جمع ہونا

## assist

madad dena     مدد دینا

## attach

munsalik karna     منسلک کرنا

## attack

hamla karna     حملہ کرنا

## attain

haasil karna     حاصل کرنا

## attempt

koshish karna     کوشش کرنا

## attend

haazir hona     حاضر ہونا

## attract

lubhaana     لُبھانا

## avoid

بچنا، گریز کرنا
bachna, gurez karna

## await

intezaar karna     انتظار کرنا

## awake

جاگنا، بیدار ہونا
jaagna, bedaar hona

# Bb

## bake

khushk pakaana     خشک پکانا

## balance

tawaazun rakhna     توازن رکھنا

## ban

pabandi lagaana     پابندی لگانا

## bandage

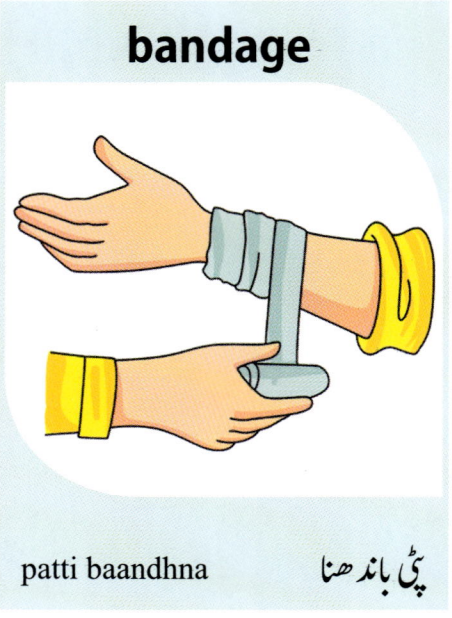

patti baandhna     پٹی باندھنا

## barbecue

گوشت کو بھوننا
gosht ko bhoonna

## bargain

sauda karna     سودا کرنا

## bark

bhonkna     بھونکنا

## bathe

nahaana     نہانا

## battle

jang ladna     جنگ لڑنا

## bear

ڈھونا، برداشت کرنا
dhona, bardaasht karna

## beat

dhol bajaana     ڈھول بجانا

## become

ho jaana       ہو جانا

## beg

maangna       مانگنا

## begin

shuroo karna       شروع کرنا

## behave

pesh aana       پیش آنا

## believe

yaqeen karna       یقین کرنا

## belong

milkiyat hona       ملکیت ہونا

## bend

jhukna       جُھکنا

## bet

shart lagaana       شرط لگانا

## beware

khabardaar hona       خبردار ہونا

## bicycle

saaikal chalaana     سائیکل چلانا

## bite

kaatna     کاٹنا

## blame

ilzaam lagaana     الزام لگانا

## bleed

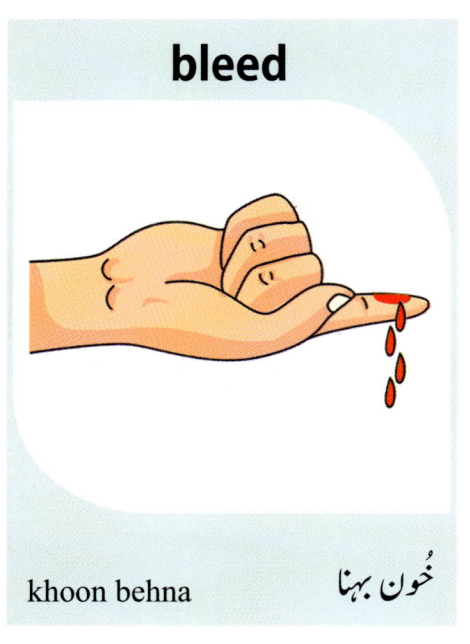

khoon behna     خُون بہنا

## blend

milaana     ملانا

## bless

duaa dena     دعا دینا

## blink

aankh jhapkaana     آنکھ جھپکانا

## block

rokna     روکنا

## bloom

bahaar par aana     بہار پر آنا

## blow

phoonk maarna     پھونک مارنا

## blow up

پھلانا، ہوا بھرنا
phulaana, hawa bharna

## blush

sharmaana     شرمانا

## board

sawaar hona     سوار ہونا

## boast

شیخی بگھارنا
shaikhi baghaarna

## boil

ubalna     اُبلنا

## book

register karna     رجسٹر کرنا

## borrow

udhaar lena     اُدھار لینا

## bother

pareshaan karna     پریشان کرنا

## bounce

uchhaalna   اُچھالنا

## bow

jhukna   جُھکنا

## bowl
*US English* **pitch**

gend phenkna   گیند پھینکنا

## box

مُکّے بازی کرنا
mukke baazi karna

## break

todna, tootna   توڑنا، ٹوٹنا

## break down

گاڑی خراب ہو جانا
gaadi kharaab ho jaana

## break in

ghus jaana   گُھس جانا

## break out

faraar ho jaana   فرار ہو جانا

## breathe

saans lena   سانس لینا

## bring

lekar aana     لیکر آنا

## bring back

waapis laana     واپس لانا

## bring up

tarbiyat karna     تربیت کرنا

## browse

ادھر ادھر سے پڑھنا
idhar udhar se parhna

## brush

برش سے صاف کرنا
brush se saaf karna

## buckle

baklas lagaana     بکلس لگانا

## budge

hataana, sarkaana     ہٹانا، سرکانا

## build

بنانا، تعمیر کرنا
banaana, tameer karna

## bully

غُنڈہ گردی کرنا
ghunda gardi karna

## bump

دھکا لگنا، دھچکا لگنا
dhakka lagna, dhachka lagna

## burn

jalaana
جلانا

## burst

phatna, phootna
پھٹنا، پھوٹنا

## bury

زمین میں دبانا
zameen mein dabaana

## button

button lagaana
بٹن لگانا

## buy

khareedna
خریدنا

# Cc

## cage

پنجرے میں قید کرنا
pinjre main qaid karna

## calculate

hisaab karna
حساب کرنا

## call

phone karna     فون کرنا

## camp

khema lagaana     خیمہ لگانا

## can

ڈبے میں بند کرنا
dibbe mein band karna

## care

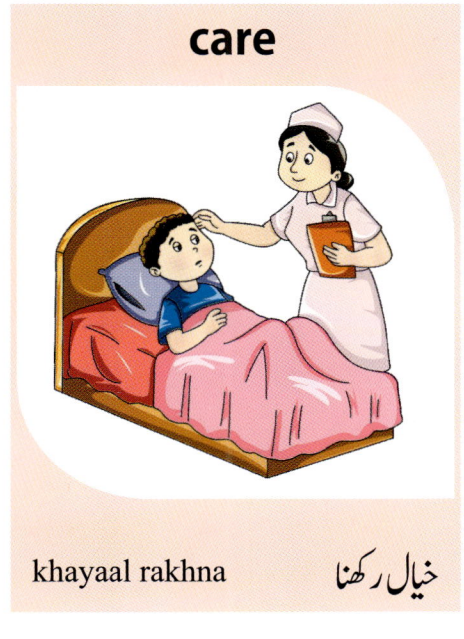

khayaal rakhna     خیال رکھنا

## carry

اٹھاکر لے جانا
uthaakar le jana

## carve

mujassima banaana     مجسمہ بنانا

## catch

pakadna, lapakna     پکڑنا، لپکنا

## catch up

پکڑنے کی کوشش کرنا
pakadne ki koshish karna

## celebrate

jashn manaana     جشن منانا

## change

badalna     بدلنا

## charge

charge karna     چارج کرنا

## chase

peechha karna     پیچھا کرنا

## chat

gap shap karna     گپ شپ کرنا

## cheat

dhoka dena     دھوکہ دینا

## check

جانچ پڑتال کرنا
jaanch padtaal karna

## check in

ہوٹل میں ٹھہرنے کے لئے آنا
hotel mein theherne ke liye aana

## check up

jaanch karna     جانچ کرنا

## cheer

khush hona     خوش ہونا

## chew

chabaana     چبانا

## chip

taraashna     تراشنا

## chirp

chehchahaana     چہچہانا

## choose

intekhaab karna     انتخاب کرنا

## chop

کاٹنا، ٹکڑے ٹکڑے کرنا
kaatna, tukde tukde karna

## chuckle

khi khi karna     کھی کھی کرنا

## circle

گول دائرہ بنانا
gol daaira banaana

## claim

haq jataana     حق جتانا

## clap

taali bajaana     تالی بجانا

## clean

safaai karna صفائی کرنا

## clear

saaf karna صاف کرنا

## click

*US English* **snap**

chutki bajaana چٹکی بجانا

## climb

upar charhna اوپر چڑھنا

## cling

chimatna چمٹنا

## clip

بالوں میں کلپ لگانا
baalon mein clip lagaana

## close

band karna بند کرنا

## cluck

kut kut karna کٹ کٹ کرنا

## coach

تعلیم دینا، سکھانا
taleem dena, sikhaana

## coil

kundal banaana كنڈل بنانا

## collapse

gir jaana گرجانا

## collect

ikaththa karna اکٹھا کرنا

## collide

takraana ٹکرانا

## colour

*US English* **color**

rang bharna رنگ بھرنا

## comb

kanghi karna کنگھی کرنا

## come

aana آنا

## come in

andar aana اندر آنا

## come out

baahar nikalna باہر نکلنا

## commence

shuroo karna شروع کرنا

## commute

safar karna سفر کرنا

## compete

muqaabla karna مقابلہ کرنا

## complain

shikaayat karna شکایت کرنا

## conduct

انتظام کرنا
intezaam karna

## connect

milaana ملانا

## consult

mashwara lena مشورہ لینا

## cook

pakaana پکانا

## cool

thanda karna ٹھنڈا کرنا

## copy

naqal karna نقل کرنا

## cough

khaansna کھانسنا

## count

ginti karna گنتی کرنا

## cover

dhakna ڈھکنا

## crack

chatakhna چٹخنا

## crash

takra jaana ٹکرا جانا

## crawl

rengna, ghisatna رینگنا، گھسٹنا

## create

تخلیق کرنا، بنانا
tahkhleeq karna, banaana

## creep

دبے پاوں چلنا
dabe paon chalna

### croak

tarrana ٹرانا

### cross

paar karna پار کرنا

### cross out

kaati lagaana کاٹی لگانا

### crouch

dabakna دبکنا

### crow

baang dena بانگ دینا

### crowd

bheer lagna بھیڑ لگنا

### crumble

reza reza karna ریزہ ریزہ کرنا

### cry

rona رونا

### cuddle

chimtaana چمٹانا

## curl

گھنگریالے بال بنانا
ghunghryale baal banaana

## cut

kaatna    کاٹنا

## cut down

kaat ke giraana    کاٹ کے گرانا

# Dd

## damage

نقصان پہنچانا
nuqsaan pohnchaana

## dance

raqs karna    رقص کرنا

## dangle

لٹکانا، ہلانا، جھلانا
latkaana, hilaana, jhulaana

## darn

rafu karna    رفو کرنا

## dash

تیزی میں حرکت کرنا
tezi mein harkat karna

## decide

faisla karna    فیصلہ کرنا

## decorate

سجانا، مزین کرنا
sajaana, muzayyan karna

## defend

bachaana    بچانا

## deliver

حوالے کرنا، سپرد کرنا
hawaale karna, supurd karna

## design

نقشہ تیار کرنا
naqsha tayyaar karna

## destroy

tabaah karna    تباہ کرنا

## dial

نمبر ملانا، ٹیلی فون کرنا
number milaana, telephone karna

## dice

چوکور شکل میں کاٹنا
chokor shakal mein kaatna

## dig

khudaai karna    کھدائی کرنا

## dip

dubona     ڈبونا

## disappear

ghaib ho jana     غائب ہو جانا

## disappoint

maayoos hona     مایوس ہونا

## discard

بیکار سمجھ کر پھینک دینا
bekaar samajh kar phenk dena

## discover

inkishaaf karna     انکشاف کرنا

## dive

dubki lagaana     ڈبکی لگانا

## divide

taqseem karna     تقسیم کرنا

## do

koi kaam karna     کوئی کام کرنا

## drag

کھینچنا، گھسیٹنا
khenchna, ghaseetna

## draw

drawing karna     ڈرائنگ کرنا

## dream

khwaab dekhna     خواب دیکھنا

## dress

kapre pehanna     کپڑے پہننا

## drift

bahe chale jaana     بہے چلے جانا

## drill

suraakh karna     سوراخ کرنا

## drink

peena     پینا

## drive

gaadi chalaana     گاڑی چلانا

## drop

پھینکنا، گرا دینا
phenkna, gira dena

## dry

khushk hona     خشک ہونا

# Ee

## earn

kamaana  کمانا

## eat

khaana  کھانا

## elect

intekhaab karna  انتخاب کرنا

## embrace

gale lagaana  گلے لگانا

## empty

khaali karna  خالی کرنا

## enclose

ihaata karna  احاطہ کرنا

## encourage

himmat afzaai karna  ہِمّت افزائی کرنا

## enjoy

lutf andoz hona  لُطف اندوز ہونا

## enter

daakhil hona داخل ہونا

## entertain

dil behlaana دل بہلانا

## erase

mitaana مٹانا

## escape

faraar hona فرار ہونا

## examine

parakhna پرکھنا

## excite

josh mein hona جوش میں ہونا

## exercise

warzish karna ورزش کرنا

## explain

tashreeh karna تشریح کرنا

## explore

کسی نئی جگہ کی سیاحت کرنا
kisi nai jaga ki siyaahat karna

# Ff

## fail

naakaam hona ناکام ہونا

## faint

behosh ho jana بے ہوش ہو جانا

## fall

girna گرنا

## fall asleep

so jana سو جانا

## feed

khilaana کھلانا

## feel

mehsoos karna محسوس کرنا

## fetch

lekar aana لے کر آنا

## fight

larna لڑنا

## fill

bharna     بھرنا

## find

dhoondna, paana     ڈھونڈنا، پانا

## fish

مچھلی کا شکار کرنا
machhli ka shikaar karna

## fit

درست آنا، فٹ آنا
durust aana, fit aana

## fix

ٹھیک کرنا
theek karna

## flap

pharpharaana     پھڑپھڑانا

## flash

bijli chamakna     بجلی چمکنا

## flee

faraar ho jaana     فرار ہو جانا

## fling

phenkna     پھینکنا

## flip

ہلکے سے اچھالنا
halke se uchhaalna

## float

tairna تیرنا

## flood

selaab aana سیلاب آنا

## fly

udna اڑنا

## fold

lapetna, tey karna لپیٹنا، تہ کرنا

## follow

peechhe jaana پیچھے جانا

## forbid

mana karna منع کرنا

## forget

bhoolna بھولنا

## freeze

jam jaana جم جانا

## frighten

daraana ڈرانا

## frown

tiyoori charhaana تیوری چڑھانا

## fry

talna تلنا

# Gg

## gain

haasil karna حاصل کرنا

## gallop

sarpat daudna سرپٹ دوڑنا

## gape

munh phaadna منہ پھاڑنا

## garden

baaghbaani karna باغبانی کرنا

## gargle

gharaara karna غرارہ کرنا

## gasp

haanpna     ہانپنا

## gather

ikaththa karna     اکٹھا کرنا

## gaze

ٹکٹکی باندھ کر دیکھنا
tiktiki baandhkar dekhna

## gesture

ishaara karna     اشارہ کرنا

## get

haasil karna     حاصل کرنا

## get across

paar karna     پار کرنا

## get down

neeche utarna     نیچے اترنا

## get dressed

tayyaar hona     تیار ہونا

## get off

utarna     اترنا

### get on

sawaar hona     سوار ہونا

### get over

paar karna     پار کرنا

### get up

اُٹھنا، جاگنا، بیدار ہونا
uthna, jaagna, bedaar hona

### giggle

کھسیانی ہنسی ہنسنا
khisyaani hansi hansna

### give

dena     دینا

### go

رخصت ہونا، روانہ ہونا
rukhsat hona, rawaana hona

### gobble

harap karna     ہڑپ کرنا

### grab

پکڑنا، ہتھیانا
pakarna, hathyaana

### grate

kaddukash karna     کدوکش کرنا

### grease

greese lagaana     گریس لگانا

### greet

خیر مقدم کرنا
khair maqdam karna

### grill

aag par senkna     آگ پر سینکنا

### grin

کھسیانی ہنسی ہنسنا
khisyaani hansi hansna

### grind

peesna     پیسنا

### grip

pakadna     پکڑنا

### grow

ugaana     اگانا

### growl

ghurraana     غرّانا

### grunt

جانور کا آواز نکالنا
jaanwar ka aawaaz nikaalna

## guard

نگہبانی کرنا
nigehbaani karna

## guess

andaaza lagaana    اندازہ لگانا

## guide

rehnumaai karna    رہنمائی کرنا

# Hh

## halt

rokna    روکنا

## halve

aadhaa karna    آدھا کرنا

## hammer

ہتھوڑا مارنا
hathauraa  maarna

## handcuff

ہتھکڑی لگانا
hathkari lagaana

## hang

latakna    لٹکنا

## harvest

fasl kaatna     فصل کاٹنا

## hatch

ande se nikalna     انڈے سے نکلنا

## hate

nafrat karna     نفرت کرنا

## heap

dher lagaana     ڈھیر لگانا

## hear

sunna     سننا

## heat

garm karna     گرم کرنا

## help

madad karna     مدد کرنا

## hide

chhupna     چھپنا

## hike

پہاڑ پر سفر پر جانا
pahaad par safar par jaana

## hiss

سی سی کی آواز کرنا
si si ki aawaaz karna

## hit

maarna — مارنا

## hoist

jhanda lehraana — جھنڈا لہرانا

## hold

pakadna — پکڑنا

## honk

گاڑی کا ہورن بجانا
gaadi ka horn bajaana

## hop

uchhalna, koodna — اچھلنا، کودنا

## host

mezbaani karna — میزبانی کرنا

## hover

mandlaana — منڈلانا

## huddle

بے ترتیب اکٹھے ہونا
betarteeb ikaththe hona

## hug

gale lagaana     گلے لگانا

## hum

bhinbhinaana     بھنبھنانا

## hurt

تکلیف پہنچانا
takleef ponhchaana

# Ii

## imagine

tasawwur karna     تصور کرنا

## injure

chot lagaana     چوٹ لگانا

## insert

andar daalna     اندر ڈالنا

## inspect

muaaena karna     معائنہ کرنا

## install

lagaana     لگانا

### instruct

پڑھانا، تعلیم دینا
parhaana, taleem dena

### interview

انٹرویو دینا
interview dena

### introduce

تعارف کرانا
taaruf karaana

### invent

eejaad karna    ایجاد کرنا

### iron

istri karna    اِستری کرنا

### itch

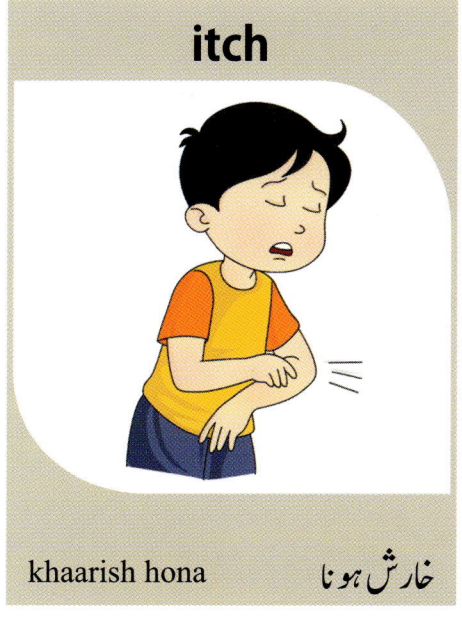

khaarish hona    خارش ہونا

### Jj

### jam

جام ہونا، پھنس جانا
jaam hona, phans jaana

### jingle

جھن جھن کرنا
jhan jhan karna

## jog

اُچھلتے ہوئے دوڑنا
uchhalte hue daurna

## join

jorna
جوڑنا

## joke

mazaaq karna
مذاق کرنا

## jolt

hichkole khaana
ہچکولے کھانا

## jostle

dhakka dena
دھکا دینا

## jot

جلدی سے کچھ لکھنا
jaldi se kuch likhna

## juggle

شعبدہ بازی دکھانا
shobda baazi dikhaana

## jumble

gadmad karna
گڈمڈ کرنا

## jump

uchhalna
اُچھلنا

# Kk

## keep

rakhna     رکھنا

## keep off

door rehna     دور رہنا

## kick

laat maarna     لات مارنا

## kindle

aag sulgaana     آگ سلگانا

## kiss

choomna     چومنا

## knead

goondhna     گوندھنا

## kneel

زمین پر گھٹنے ٹیکنا
zameen par ghutne tekna

## knit

bunna     بُننا

## knock

دستک دینا، کھٹکھٹانا
dastak dena, khatkhataana

## knock down

maar giraana مار گرانا

## know

ilm hona علم ہونا

# Ll

## land

zameen par utarna زمین پر اترنا

## laugh

hansna ہنسنا

## lay

ande dena انڈے دینا

## lead

rehnumaai karna رہنمائی کرنا

## leak

risna رسنا

## lean

sahaara lena     سہارا لینا

## leap

اچھلنا، کودنا
uchhalna, koodna

## learn

seekhna     سیکھنا

## leave

چھوڑنا، روانہ ہونا
chhorna, rawaana hona

## lend

qarz dena     قرض دینا

## let go

jaane dena     جانے دینا

## let in

aane dena     آنے دینا

## lie

letna     لیٹنا

## lift

uthaana     اٹھانا

## light

jalaana      جلانا

## like

pasand karna      پسند کرنا

## listen

sunna      سننا

## load

maal laadna      مال لادنا

## lock

taala lagaana      تالا لگانا

## look

dekhna      دیکھنا

## loosen

dheela hona      ڈھیلا ہونا

## lose

khona      کھونا

## love

mohabbat karna      محبت کرنا

# Mm

## mail

daak bhejna · ڈاک بھیجنا

## make

banaana · بنانا

## manufacture

بنانا، تیار کرنا
banaana, tayyaar karna

## march

قدم ملا کر چلنا
qadam milaakr chalna

## mark

nishaan lagaana · نشان لگانا

## marry

شادی کرنا
shaadi karna

## mash

maleeda banaana · ملیدہ بنانا

## match

mel khaana · میل کھانا

## measure

پیمائش کرنا
paimaaish karna

## meet

mulaaqaat karna  ملاقات کرنا

## melt

pighalna  پگھلنا

## mend

اصلاح کرنا، مرمت کرنا
islaah karna, marammat karna

## mew

میاؤں میاؤں کرنا
miyaon miyaon karna

## milk

doodh dohna  دودھ دوہنا

## mime

خاموش مزاحیہ ایکٹنگ کرنا
khaamosh mizaahiyya acting karna

## mince

qeema banaana  قیمہ بنانا

## mix

milaana  ملانا

## model

model banna     ماڈل بننا

## mop

pochha lagaana     پوچھا لگانا

## mount

upar charhna     اوپر چڑھنا

## move

jaga se hataana     جگہ سے ہٹانا

## mow

ghaas kaatna     گھاس کاٹنا

## munch

چبر چبر چبانا
chabar chabar chabaana

# Nn

## nail

keel thokna     کیل ٹھوکنا

## name

naam rakhna     نام رکھنا

## nap

jhapki lena جھپکی لینا

## neigh

گھوڑے کا ہنہنانا
ghode ka hinhinaana

## net

jaal daalna جال ڈالنا

## nibble

kutarna کترنا

## nip

چٹکی لینا، کاٹنا
chutki lena, kaatna

## nod

سر کو ہلانا
sar ko hilaana

## notice

tawajjuh karna توجہ کرنا

## nudge

kohni maarna کہنی مارنا

## nurse

تیمارداری کرنا
teemaardaari karna

# Oo

## obey

kehna maanna     کہنا ماننا

## occupy

سیٹ پر قبضہ کرنا
seat par qabza karna

## offer

pesh karna     پیش کرنا

## oil

tel daalna     تیل ڈالنا

## open

kholna     کھولنا

## operate

machine chalaana     مشین چلانا

## order

order dena     آرڈر دینا

## overtake

aage nikalna     آگے نکلنا

## overturn

palat jaana     پلٹ جانا

## owe

maqrooz hona     مقروض ہونا

## own

maalik hona     مالک ہونا

# Pp

## pack

سامان پیک کرنا
saamaan pack karna

## paddle

کشتی چلانا
kashti chalaana

## paint

roghan karna     روغن کرنا

## park

گاڑی کھڑی کرنا
gaadi khadi karna

## part

alag alag hona     الگ الگ ہونا

## pass

دوسرے کو دینا
doosre ko dena

## paste

chipkaana چپکانا

## pat

thapki dena تھپکی دینا

## patch

pewand lagaana پیوند لگانا

## patrol

gasht lagaana گشت لگانا

## pave

راستہ ہموار کرنا
raasta hamwaar karna

## paw

panja maarna پنجہ مارنا

## pay

ada karna ادا کرنا

## peck

chonchein maarna چونچیں مارنا

## pedal

سائیکل کا پیڈل مارنا
saaikal ka pedal maarna

## peel

chheelna چھیلنا

## peep

jhaankna جھانکنا

## peg

کپڑوں میں چٹکی لگانا
kapdon mein chutki lagaana

## perch

شاخ پر بیٹھنا
shaakh par baithna

## perform

اداکاری کرنا، انجام دینا
adaakaari karna, anjaam dena

## phone

telephone karna ٹیلیفون کرنا

## photograph

tasweer khenchna تصویر کھینچنا

## pick

chunna, uthaana چننا، اٹھانا

## pick up

uthaana     اٹھانا

## picnic

tafreeh ko jaana     تفریح کو جانا

## pierce

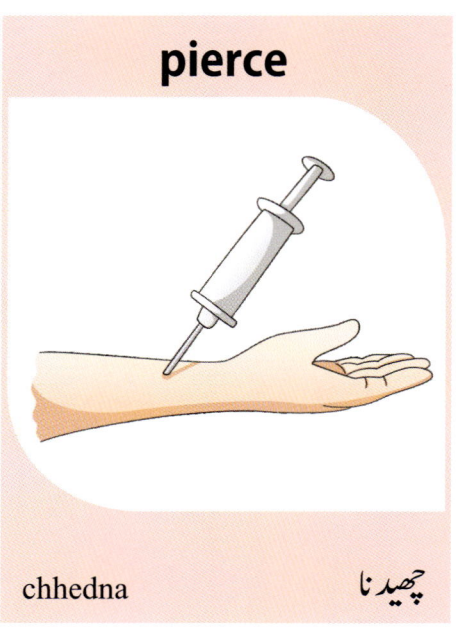

chhedna     چھیدنا

## pile

dher lagaana     ڈھیر لگانا

## pin

pin lagaana     پن لگانا

## pinch

chutki lena     چٹکی لینا

## place

jagah par rakhna     جگہ پر رکھنا

## plan

programm banaana     پروگرام بنانا

## plant

pauda lagaana     پودا لگانا

## play

khelna

کھیلنا

## plough

hal chalaana

ہل چلانا

## pluck

پھل یا پھول توڑنا
phal ya phool todna

## plug

بجلی کا پلگ لگانا
bijli ka plug lagaana

## point

ishaara karna

اشارہ کرنا

## poke

chubhona

چبھونا

## polish

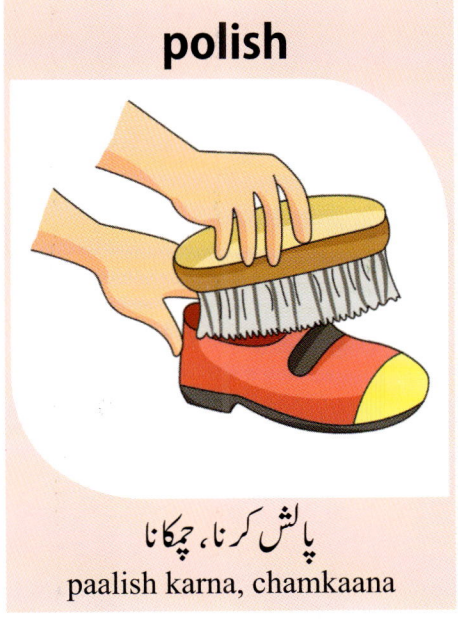

پالش کرنا، چمکانا
paalish karna, chamkaana

## pollute

آلودہ کرنا، گندا کرنا
aalooda karna, ganda karna

## pose

andaaz banaana

انداز بنانا

## pour

برتن میں انڈیلنا
bartan mein undelna

## powder

powder lagaana   پوڈر لگانا

## praise

tareef karna   تعریف کرنا

## pray

duaa karna   دعا کرنا

## press

dabaana   دبانا

## print

چھاپنا، طبع کرنا
chhaapna, tabaa karna

## protect

hifaazat karna   حفاظت کرنا

## pull

khenchna   کھینچنا

## pump

پمپ سے ہوا بھرنا
pump se hawa bharna

### punch

mukka maarna     مکّا مارنا

### punish

sazaa dena     سزا دینا

### push

dhakelna     دھکیلنا

# Qq

### quack

بطخ کا قائیں قائیں کرنا
battakh ka qaaen qaaen karna

### quarrel

ladna, jhagadna     لڑنا، جھگڑنا

### quarter

چار ٹکڑوں میں بانٹنا
chaar tukdon mein baantna

### quench

pyaas bujhaana     پیاس بجھانا

### question

sawaal karna     سوال کرنا

### queue

قطار باندھنا
qataar baandhna

### quit

chhor dena چھوڑ دینا

### quiz

sawaal puchhna سوال پوچھنا

# Rr

### race

دوڑ کا مقابلہ کرنا
daur ka muqaabla karna

### rain

baarish hona بارش ہونا

### raise

uthaana اٹھانا

### rake

جیلی سے اکٹھا کرنا
jeeli se ikaththa karna

### ram

zor se takraana زور سے ٹکرانا

## reach

pohonchna     پہونچنا

## read

parhna     پڑھنا

## receive

lena     لینا

## recline

tek lagaana     ٹیک لگانا

## record

آواز کو مشین میں ریکارڈ کرنا
aawaaz ko masheen mein record karna

## recycle

دوبارہ استعمال میں لانا
dobaara istemaal mein laana

## reflect

منعکس ہونا
munakis hona

## refuse

inkaar karna     انکار کرنا

## release

aazaad karna     آزاد کرنا

## remember

yaad aana     یاد کرنا

## repair

marammat karna     مرمت کرنا

## report

ittelaa dena     اطلاع دینا

## request

darkhwaast karna     درخواست کرنا

## rescue

bachaana     بچانا

## respect

izzat karna     عزت کرنا

## rest

aaraam karna     آرام کرنا

## return

waapis karna     واپس کرنا

## ride

sawaari karna     سواری کرنا

### ring

ghanti bajaana غھنٹی بجانا

### ring up

telephone karna ٹیلیفون کرنا

### rinse

khangaalna کھنگالنا

### rip

kapre ka phatna کپڑے کا پھٹنا

### rise

tuloo hona طلوع ہونا

### risk

خطرے کا کام کرنا
khatre ka kaam karna

### roar

dahaadna دہاڑنا

### roast

bhoonna بھوننا

### rock

jhulaana جھلانا

## roll

lapetna لپیٹنا

## row

kashti chalaana کشتی چلانا

## rub

رگڑنا، مسلنا
ragarna, masalna

## ruffle

بال خراب کرنا، پریشان کرنا
baal kharaab karna, pareshaan karna

## ruin

kharaab karna خراب کرنا

## run

bhaagna بھاگنا

## run after

peechha karna پیچھا کرنا

## run into

takraana ٹکرانا

## rush

tezi se jaana تیزی سے جانا

# Ss

## sag

وزن کی وجہ سے جھک جانا
wazn ki wajah se jhuk jaana

## sail

سمندر کا سفر کرنا
samandar ka safar karna

## salute

salaami dena     سلامی دینا

## save

محفوظ کرنا، بچا کر رکھنا
mehfooz karna, bachaa kar rakhna

## scare

daraana     ڈرانا

## scold

daantna     ڈانٹنا

## scoop

کفچے سے نکالنا
kafcha se nikaalna

## score

اسکور کرنا، نمبر لینا
score karna, number lena,

## scratch

khujaana · کھجانا

## scratch out

یونہی لائنیں بنانا
yoonhi lainen banaana

## scream

cheekh maarna · چیخ مارنا

## screw

pench lagaana · پینچ لگانا

## scrub

رگڑ کر صاف کرنا
ragad kar saaf karna

## seal

mohar lagaana · مہر لگانا

## see

dekhna · دیکھنا

## seek

تلاش کرنا
talaash karna

## select

منتخب کرنا
muntakhab karna

## sell

farokht karna     فروخت کرنا

## send

bhejna     بھیجنا

## separate

alag alag karna     الگ الگ کرنا

## serve

پیش کرنا
pesh karna

## set

theek bithaana     ٹھیک بٹھانا

## sew

seena     سینا

## shade

chhaon karna     چھاؤں کرنا

## shake

hilaana     ہلانا

## shape

shakal dena     شکل دینا

## share

baantna
بانٹنا

## sharpen

چھیلنا، تیز کرنا
chheelna, tez karna

## shave

بال صاف کرنا
baal saaf karna

## shear

kaatna, mondna
کاٹنا، مونڈنا

## shell

chhilka utaarna
چھلکا اتارنا

## shelter

panaah lena
پناہ لینا

## shift

muntaqil karna
منتقل کرنا

## shine

chamakna
چمکنا

## shiver

کانپنا، تھرتھرانا
kaanpna, thartharaana

## shoot

nishaana lagaana نشانہ لگانا

## shop

khareedaari karna خریداری کرنا

## shout

cheekhna چیخنا

## shovel

belche se hataana بیلچے سے ہٹانا

## show

dikhaana دکھانا

## shower

فوارے سے نہانا
fawwaare se nahaana

## shut

band karna بند کرنا

## sign

dastkhat karna دستخط کرنا

## signal

ishaara dena اشارہ دینا

## sing

gaana     گانا

## sink

doobna     ڈوبنا

## sip

chuski lagaana     چسکی لگانا

## sit

baithna     بیٹھنا

## skate board

برفانی کھڑاوٗں سے پھسنا
barfaani khadhaaon se phisalna,

## ski

shi par phisalna     شی پر پھسلنا

## skid

phisalna     پھسلنا

## skip

rassi koodna     رسی کودنا

## slap

طمانچہ مارنا
tamaancha maarna

### slash

kaat daalna     کاٹ ڈالنا

### sledge

phisalna     پھسلنا

### sleep

sona     سونا

### slice

پتلے پتلے ٹکڑے کاٹنا
patle patle tukre kaatna

### slide

phisalna     پھسلنا

### slip

phisal jaana     پھسل جانا

### slip under

andar sarkaana     اندر سرکانا

### smash

tor phor daalna     توڑ پھوڑ ڈالنا

### smell

soonghna     سونگھنا

## smile

muskuraana     مسکرانا

## snatch

chheenna     چھیننا

## sneeze

chheenkna     چھینکنا

## sniff

soonghna     سونگھنا

## snore

kharraate lena     خرّاٹے لینا

## snorkel

سانس لینے والی ٹیوب کے ساتھ تیرنا
saans lene wali tube ke sath tairna

## snow

barf parna     برف پڑنا

## soak

bhigona     بھگونا

## soar

اونچائی پر اڑنا
oonchaai par udna

## sob

siskiyaan bharna سسکیاں بھرنا

## sort

chhaantna چھانٹنا

## sow

bona بونا

## sparkle

chamakna چمکنا

## speak

bolna بولنا

## spill

bikharna بکھرنا

## spit

thookna تھوکنا

## splash

چھپ چھپ کرنا
chhap chhap karna

## spoil

خراب کرنا، بگاڑنا
kharaab karna, bigaarna

### spray
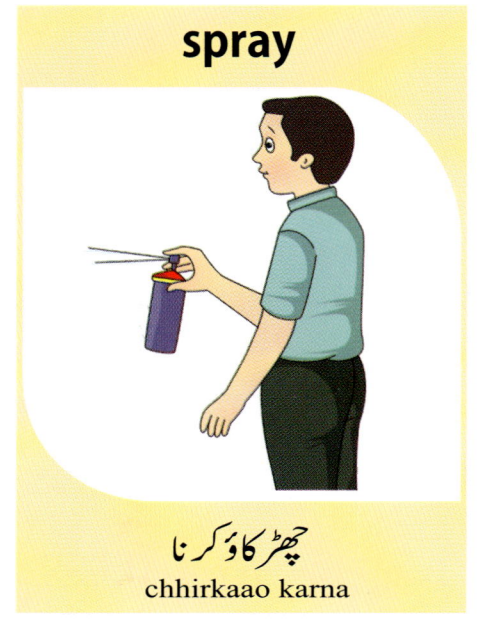
چھڑ کاؤ کرنا
chhirkaao karna

### spread

phailaana
پھیلانا

### spring

koodna
کودنا

### sprinkle

chhirakna
چھڑ کنا

### spy

jaasoosi karna
جاسوسی کرنا

### squash

nichodna
نچوڑنا

### squat

آلتی پالتی مار کر بیٹھنا
aalti paalti maarkar baithna

### squeeze

بھینچنا، رس نکالنا
bheenchna, ras nikaalna

### stack

dher lagaana
ڈھیر لگانا

### stamp

mohar lagaana     مہر لگانا

### stand

khara hona     کھڑا ہونا

### stand back

پیچھے کھڑا ہونا
peechhe khara hona

### stand up

khara ho jaana     کھڑا ہو جانا

### stare

ghoorna     گھورنا

### start

shuroo karna     شروع کرنا

### stay

قیام کرنا
qayaam karna

### stay away

door rehna     دور رہنا

### steal

chori karna     چوری کرنا

## steam

بھاپ کا نکلنا
bhaanp ka nikalna

## step

قدم رکھنا
qadam rakhna

## stick

chipkaana
چپکانا

## sting

ڈنک مارنا، کاٹنا
dank maarna, kaatna

## stink

badboo dena
بدبو دینا

## stir

harkat dena
حرکت دینا

## stitch

seena
سینا

## stomp

زور سے قدم پر مارنا
zor se qadam par maarna

## stoop

jhukna
جھکنا

### stop

رکنا     rukna

### store

محفوظ کرنا، جمع کرنا
mehfooz karna, jama karna

### stretch

khenchana     کھینچنا

### strike

ضرب لگانا
zarb lagaana

### string

dori mein pirona     ڈوری میں پرونا

### stroke

ہاتھ پھیرنا، سہلانا
haath pherna, sehlaana

### study

مطالعہ کرنا
mutaala karna

### subtract

Ghataana     گھٹانا

### support

sahaara dena     سہارا دینا

### surf

پانی کی سطح پر تیرنا
paani ki satah par tairna

### surprise

hairaan kar dena حیران کر دینا

### swallow

nigalna نگلنا

### sweat

paseena aana پسینہ آنا

### sweep

جھاڑو لگانا، صاف کرنا
jhaaru lagaana, saaf karna

### swell

soojna سوجنا

### swim

tairna تیرنا

### swing

jhoolna جھولنا

### swipe

swipe karna سوائپ کرنا

# Tt

## take

lena    لینا

## take off

oopar uthna    اوپر اٹھنا

## talk

بات چیت کرنا
baatcheet karna

## tame
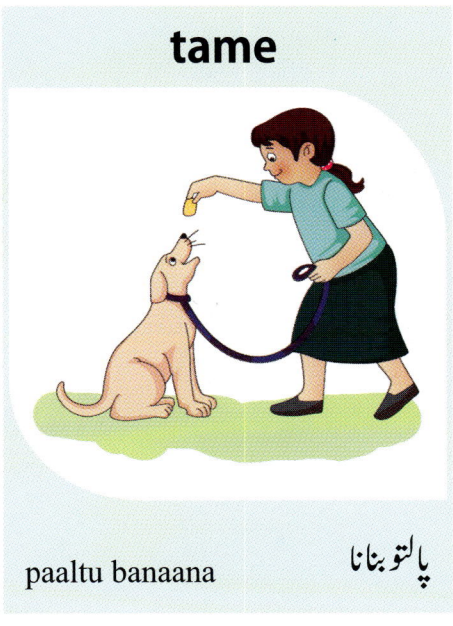

paaltu banaana    پالتو بنانا

## tap

پاؤں زمین پر مارنا
paaon zameen par maarna

## taste

chakhna    چکھنا

## teach

taleem dena    تعلیم دینا

## tear

phaarna    پھاڑنا

## tell

bataana, kehna     بتانا، کہنا

## test

jaeza lena     جائزہ لینا

## thank

shukriya ada karna     شکریہ ادا کرنا

## think

سوچنا، خیال کرنا
sochna, khayaal karna

## thread

dhaaga daalna     دھاگا ڈالنا

## throw

phenkna     پھینکنا

## throw away

phenk dena     پھینک دینا

## tick

صحیح کی علامت لگانا
sahih ki alaamat lagaana

## tickle

gudgudi karna     گدگدی کرنا

## tidy

صاف ستھرا کرنا
saaf suthra karna

## tie

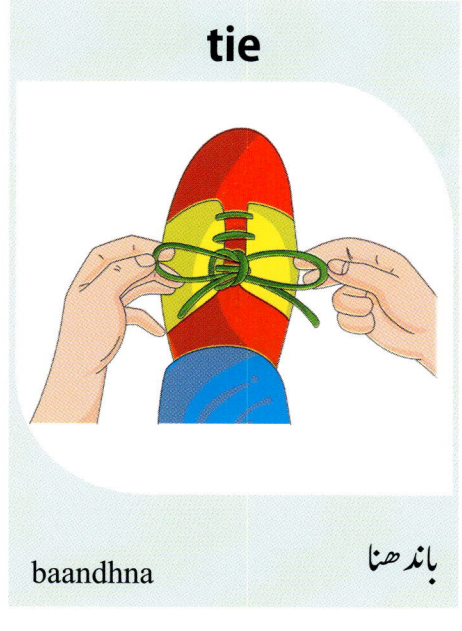

باندھنا
baandhna

## tighten

کس کر باندھنا
kas kas kar baandhna

## time

وقت کی منصوبہ بندی کرنا
waqt ki mansooba bandi karna

## tip

بخشش دینا
bakhshish dena

## tiptoe

دبے پاؤں چلنا
dabe paaon chalna

## toast

روٹی سینکنا
roti senkna

## toss

سکّہ اچھالنا
sikka uchhaalna

## touch

چھونا
chhoona

### touch down

جہاز کا زمین پر اترنا
jahaaz ka zameen par utarna

### tour

siyaahat karna     سیاحت کرنا

### tow

گاڑی کو کھینچنا
gaadi ko khenchna

### train

tarbiyat dena     تربیت دینا

### trap

جال میں پھانسنا
jaal mein phaansna

### travel

safar karna     سفر کرنا

### tremble

لرزنا، کانپنا
larazna, kaanpna

### trick

کرتب یا کھیل دکھانا
kartab ya khel dikhaana

### trim

کانٹ چھانٹ کرنا
kaat chhaant karna

## trot

گھوڑے کا دلکی چلانا
ghode ka dulki chalaana

## try

koshish karna کوشش کرنا

## tug

zor se khenchna زور سے کھینچنا

## turn

morna موڑنا

## turn off

band karna بند کرنا

## turn on

kholna کھولنا

## twinkle

ٹمٹمانا، جگمگانا
timtimaana, jagmagaana

## twist

marorna مروڑنا

## type

type karna ٹائپ کرنا

# U u

## understand

samajhna — سمجھنا

## unload

maal utaarna — مال اتارنا

## unlock

taala kholna — تالا کھولنا

## unpack

saamaan kholna — سامان کھولنا

## untie

girah kholna — گرہ کھولنا

## unwrap

kaghaz ka packet kholna — کاغذ کا پیکٹ کھولنا

## upset

mayoos hona — مایوس ہونا

## use

istemaal karna — استعمال کرنا

# Vv

### vacate

khaali karna   خالی کرنا

### vacuum

گرد کش سے صفائی کرنا
gardkush se safaai karna

### value

qeemat lagaana   قیمت لگانا

### vanish

ghaaib hona   غائب ہونا

### vibrate

مرتعش ہونا، ارتعاش پیدا کرنا
murtaish hona, irtiaash paida karna

### view

dekhna   دیکھنا

### visit

ملنے آنا یا جانا
milne aana ya jaana

### voice

aawaaz lagaana   آواز لگانا

## volunteer

رضاکارانہ کام کرنا
razaakaaraana kaam karna

## vote

vote daalna    ووٹ ڈالنا

## vow

عہد کرنا، قسم کھانا
ahed karna, qasam khaana

# Ww

## waddle

جھومتے جھامتے چلنا
jhoomte jhaamte chalna

## wade

پانی سے ہو کر گزرنا
paani se hokar guzarna

## wag

ادھر ادھر ہلانا
idhar udhar hilaana

## wait

intezaar karna    انتظار کرنا

## wake

بیدار ہونا
bedaar hona

## wake up

bedaar karna     بیدار کرنا

## walk

paidal chalna     پیدل چلنا

## walk away

chhorkar jaana     چھوڑ کر جانا

## wander

ادھر ادھر پھرنا، مارا مارا پھرنا
idhar udhar phirna, maara maara phirna

## want

چاہنا، خواہش رکھنا
chaahna, khwaahish rakhna

## warm

garm karna     گرم کرنا

## warn

خبردار کرنا
khabardaar karna

## wash

dhona     دھونا

## waste

zaae karna     ضائع کرنا

## watch

دیکھنا، مشاہدہ کرنا

dekhna, mushahada karna

## water

پانی دینا

paani dena

## wave

ہاتھ ہلاکر اشارہ کرنا

hath hilaakar ishaara karna

## wear

pehenna          پہننا

## wear out

استعمال سے خراب ہو جانا

istemaal se kharaab ho jaana

## weave

bunna          بننا

## weed

گھاس پھوس ہٹانا

ghaas phoos hataana

## weep

rona          رونا

## weigh

wazn karna          وزن کرنا

## welcome

خیر مقدم کرنا
khair maqdam karna

## wet

geela ho jaana  گیلا ہو جانا

## wheel

پہیہ دار کرسی لے جانا
pahiyyadaar kursi le jaana

## whip

phentna  پھینٹنا

## whisper

sargoshi karna  سرگوشی کرنا

## whistle

seeti bajaana  سیٹی بجانا

## win

فتح حاصل کرنا
fateh haasil karna

## wind

chaabi ghumaana  چابی گھمانا

## wink

aankh maarna  آنکھ مارنا

## wipe

ponchhna پونچھنا

## wish

aarzoo karna آرزو کرنا

## wobble

dagmagaana ڈگمگانا

## wonder

حیران ہونا
hairaan hona

## work

kaam karna کام کرنا

## work out

warzish karna ورزش کرنا

## worry

pareshaan hona پریشان ہونا

## wrap

کاغذ میں لپیٹنا
kaaghaz mein lapetna

## wrestle

kushti larna کشتی لڑنا

## wriggle

بل کھانا، بل دینا

bal khaana, bal dena

## wring

مروڑنا، نچوڑنا

marorna, nichorna

## write

لکھنا

likhna

# Xx

## xerox

فوٹوکاپی کرنا

photocopy karna

## x-ray

ایکس رے لینا

x-ray lena

# Yy

## yank

جھٹکے کے ساتھ کھینچنا

jhatke ke saath khenchna

## yap

کتے یا پلے کا پیں پیں کرنا

kutte ya pille ka peen peen karna

91

## yawn

jamaai lena جمائی لینا

## yearn

آرزو کرنا
aarzoo karna

## yell

cheekhna چیخنا

## yelp

bhaunkna بھونکنا

## yield

فصل ہونا، پیداوار ہونا
fasl hona, paidaawaar hona

## yodel

اونچی آواز سے گانا
oonchi aawaaz se gaana

## Zz

## zigzag

ٹیڑھے میڑھے راستہ پر چلنا
terhe merhe raaste par chalna

## zoom

گاڑی کو تیزی سے چلانا
gaadhi ko tezi se chalaana